Social Conditions in Britain
1918–1939

LANCASTER PAMPHLETS

Social Conditions in Britain 1918–1939

Stephen Constantine

METHUEN · LONDON AND NEW YORK

First published in 1983 by
Methuen & Co. Ltd
11 New Fetter Lane,
London EC4P 4EE

Published in the USA by
Methuen & Co.
in association with Methuen, Inc.
733 Third Avenue, New York,
NY 10017

© *1983 Stephen Constantine*

Typeset in Great Britain by
Scarborough Typesetting Services
and printed by
Richard Clay (The Chaucer Press)
Bungay, Suffolk

British Library Cataloguing in
Publication Data

Constantine, Stephen
Social conditions in Britain, 1918–1939.
— (Lancaster pamphlets)
1. Great Britain — Social conditions —
20th century
I. Title   II. Series
941.083   HN385
ISBN 0–416–36010–6

Contents

Foreword

Lancaster Pamphlets offer concise and up-to-date accounts of major historical topics, primarily for the help of students preparing for Advanced Level examinations, though they should also be of value to those pursuing introductory courses in universities and other institutions of higher education. They do not rely on prior textbook knowledge. Without being all-embracing, their aims are to bring some of the central themes or problems confronting students and teachers into sharper focus than the textbook writer can hope to do; to provide the reader with some of the results of recent research which the textbook may not embody; and to stimulate thought about the whole interpretation of the topic under discussion. They are written by experienced university scholars who have a strong interest in teaching.

At the end of this pamphlet is a numbered list of the recent or fairly recent works that the writer considers most relevant to his subject. Where a statement or a paragraph is particularly indebted to one or more of these works, the number is given in the text in brackets. This serves at the same time to acknowledge the writer's source and to show the reader where he may find a more detailed exposition of the point concerned.

Social Conditions in Britain 1918–1939

Introduction

It is difficult for the student of interwar Britain not to have some preconceptions of the period in mind when tackling the topic of social conditions. The 1920s and 1930s still seem close to us. Impressions of these years are readily recalled by those who lived through them. A wealth of novels, plays and social commentaries first published between the wars are still in print and in wide circulation. The physical remains of the age also survive in, for example, the houses, factories and public buildings constructed at the time. Visual records too exist, richer for this period than for any earlier, thanks to the explosion in the craze for amateur photography and extensions in the techniques of cheap reproduction of photographs in books and newspapers. Moreover, this is an age which still moves before our eyes, in the documentary, newsreel and feature films made between the wars.

Out of this material from the past our impressions of interwar social conditions may unwittingly be formed. In the popular view, these years and especially the 1930s were a time of unbroken depression, deprivation and decay. It is an image coloured in dark tones, a palette made up of dole queues, hunger marches, slum houses, malnutrition and bitter class and industrial relations. Sometimes these bleak impressions of the past have been consciously and more recently evoked, because the period remains a reference point in many of our own contemporary political arguments. No discussion of unemployment in the 1980s seems complete without

1

a comparison with the depression in the 1930s. The Trades Union Congress once adopted as a campaign cry 'Forward to the 80s not back to the 30s'.

There are, however, other tantalizing if perhaps subordinate, images of interwar Britain in the modern memory which seem difficult to reconcile with a sombre portrait, brighter colours suggesting unprecedented affluence, happier innovations. Photographs suggest a people, even a working class, better dressed than their parents and grandparents before the First World War. New housing estates come to mind, rich with gardens. Between the wars the motor car became common enough to generate traffic jams and to require the building of expensive by-passes. There are impressions of holiday-makers crowding beaches. This appears, too, as the age of the mighty Wurlitzer organ, when cinemas were built as dream palaces in most towns in the country. Interwar Britain gave us the BBC, Henry Hall's Dance Band, perhaps the birth of 'pop' music. There are hints here of rising living standards.

Aware of these elements, historians have for many years been critical of the grim one-sided version of interwar social history. Indeed, some recent work has tended to take on balance a distinctly optimistic view of social conditions, identifying and explaining substantial improvements. It is the purpose of this pamphlet to take note of this research and by analysing some selected major topics to suggest how the realities which lie behind conflicting images of the period may perhaps be reconciled.

Employment and unemployment

It is useful to begin a study of social conditions by an examination of interwar employment history. Work obviously provided most families with the income which determined their standard of living. Working conditions also significantly affected the quality of life of the employed population since they spent so many hours each week at their place of work. Moreover, work provided most people with their status in society, their self-esteem and many of their social contacts. We therefore need to know what the opportunities were for employment between the wars. What mattered

2

was not just whether people were employed or unwillingly un-employed, but also in what occupations people found work and where.

The regular census of population is a good guide, in spite of the unfortunate gap in the sequence caused by the cancellation during the war of the census due to be held in 1941. What we discover are remarkable changes in the occupational distribution of the labour force, that is, in the kind of work people did for a living. Although Britain at the beginning of the twentieth century already had a highly developed economy, this was still a society in which major developments were taking place, and the pace of change acceler-ated between the wars, substantially affecting opportunities for employment. For example, until the close of the nineteenth century, manual labour had been the blessing or the curse of the vast majority of British workers. Even in 1911 about 13.7m. or 74.6 per cent of the occupied population of Great Britain were manual workers, and the absolute number grew with the rise in population to total 14.8m. manual workers in 1931. But as a per-centage of the labour force they declined to 70.3 per cent in 1931 and to 64.2 per cent by 1951. Even by 1939 the labour force had become far less dominated by manual workers than in the past. The expanding group was not made up of independent employers: in the first few decades of the century they remained with about the same share of the occupied population, 6.7 per cent in 1931. The astonishing growth was in the number of white-collar or so-called non-manual workers. They totalled 3.4m. or 18.7 per cent of the labour force in 1911, 4.8m. or 23.0 per cent in 1931 and 6.9m. or 30.9 per cent in 1951. Already by the end of the 1930s they constituted over a quarter of the labour force.

This expansion of white-collar occupations is characteristic of advanced industrial societies. It reflected an increase in the number of salary-earning industrial managers and top administrators as businesses and central and local government services expanded in size and complexity. It reflected also a shift towards a more scientifically-based industrial technology which required modern companies like Imperial Chemical Industries, formed in 1926, to recruit more technicians. There was an increased need and willing-ness to pay for the services of professional people like consultant

3

engineers, accountants, doctors and teachers. Large numbers were also joining an expanding retail sector as salesmen and shop assistants, working not only for single businesses but increasingly for the chain stores like Woolworth's and Marks and Spencer's. Boots had established 1180 branches by 1938. However, most substantial was the growth in the number of clerks, from 832,000 in 1911 or 4.5 per cent of the labour force to 1,404,000 or 6.7 per cent by 1931 and up to 2,341,000 or 10.4 per cent by 1951. Large bureaucracies were developing in industry and in government, employing large numbers of low-grade administrators, clerical officers and typists. More people found employment in such careers between the wars (7).

There were equally striking changes among the ranks of manual workers. Not only did their numbers decline as a proportion of the labour force, but economic change substantially affected their distribution between different industries. Nineteenth-century Britain had come to be dominated by a handful of major industries, especially coalmining, textiles, iron and steel production and shipbuilding. These industries grew to employ large numbers of workers. But between the wars these Victorian staple industries shrank and in the process shed workers. The number of coalminers employed in the United Kingdom fell from 1,083,000 in 1920 to 675,000 by 1938, cotton workers went down from 534,000 to 302,000, those in iron and steel from 527,000 to 342,000 and in shipbuilding from 282,000 to 129,000. We might also note the continuing decline in employment in an industry once more important than all others: the number of workers in agriculture and forestry fell from 1,661,000 to 1,221,000. But while opportunities declined in some trades, openings for manual workers grew in others. There were expanding industries which recruited additional labour. Companies making motor cars like Morris and Austin shifted to mass production techniques after 1922, and the number of workers in the vehicle industry then grew from 227,000 in 1920 to 516,000 by 1938. The Central Electricity Board was established in 1926, and thereafter the development of the national grid system increased jobs in the making and distribution of electricity. Employment in the public services of electricity, gas and water rose from 185,000 to 291,000. The stimulus

4

of improved electricity supply also helped the expansion in electrical engineering, and the number of workers in the industry went up from 171,000 to 326,000. There were also substantial increases in the number of building workers especially in the 1930s and in the distributive trades. Noticeable, if more modest, additions were made to the number of workers in the chemical, rayon, and food and drink industries. Changes in employment opportunities for manual workers must therefore be seen in terms of redeployment and not simply in terms of decline (6).

These interwar changes in the occupational structure had a particular significance for women. It is true that the number of women going out to work scarcely changed as a proportion of the number of women in the population of working age. The figures are 35.3 per cent in 1911, 34.2 per cent in 1931 and 34.7 per cent in 1951. The percentage of single women working was quite high, but social conventions still strictly limited the employment prospects of married women. Most chose to or had to give up work on marriage. Nevertheless, the actual numbers of women at work did increase from roughly 5.2m. in 1911 to 6.3m. in 1931 and to 7.0m. in 1951. There were also important changes in the kind of work women did. For example, far fewer of them were employed as textile workers, in the clothing trades or in domestic service by the end of the 1930s. Instead many more women had become for the first time firmly established in white-collar occupations, albeit usually in the more humble grades. Their intrusion into shops and offices had been accelerated by the First World War when men were recruited into the forces and women had taken their places (7).

The net effect of these occupational changes was to keep in employment the vast majority of those who explicitly sought work between the wars. This fact must always be remembered when assessing interwar social conditions. The total in civil employment in the United Kingdom was to drop from about 19.5m. in 1920 to 17.4m. in 1921, but it then rose with only a setback in the early 1930s to leave 21.8m. in work by 1939. The National Government had some justification for a complacent announcement in their election manifesto in 1935 that 'more persons are now employed in this country than ever before in its whole history'.

Nevertheless, against that substantial achievement we must now set the undeniable evidence that levels of unemployment between the wars were unusually high. Unemployment figures before the First World War are normally calculated as a percentage of that small proportion of the workforce organized in trade unions, mainly skilled and semi-skilled workers not so liable to unemployment as the unskilled. They show an average unemployment rate of 4.8 per cent for the period 1881 to 1913. Interwar figures are normally expressed as a percentage of those workers covered by unemployment insurance, and from 1920 that embraced most manual workers, including the unskilled, and other employees earning less than £250 a year. The average rate recorded from 1921 to 1939 was 14 per cent. In spite of the different statistical bases, the comparison shows a substantially higher level of unemployment between the wars than in the previous generation.

Part of the explanation lies in the violent oscillations in the trade cycle which heavily scarred interwar economic activity. A pattern of boom and slump had, of course, been a feature of nineteenth-century British industrial history. In periods of boom, sales were high, investment rose and workers were in demand, but at intervals of about eight to ten years sales fell, investment slackened and many workers lost their jobs. This business cycle was not due to factors operating solely within Great Britain: this was an economy peculiarly vulnerable to booms and slumps overseas. Britain had developed a heavy dependence on overseas markets. The output of more than one British worker in every four was sold abroad in the decade before the First World War. Such major industries as textiles, iron and steel, coal and shipbuilding were heavily dependent on these sales. Inevitably a fall in foreign demand would hit those industries, and since so many other industries relied upon their prosperity for their own sales, a depression in the export industries hit other sectors of the economy also. This sequence was repeated after the First World War. It returned, however, with exceptional severity. Soon after the war the failure of Britain's exports to recover burst a speculative boom, demand fell and unemployment rose to a peak of 16.9 per cent of insured workers in 1921. Later, as the war-damaged

European economies recovered and their purchases increased, Britain experienced through the 1920s a slow recovery. But the world economy was unstable. Countries in Latin America, Africa and Asia producing primary products like food and raw materials found the prices of their exports falling, and their earnings and consequently their purchasing power declined. This was already damaging international trade before the Wall Street stock market boom burst in October 1929 and devastated economic activity in the United States. A fall in American demand inevitably hit British business across the Atlantic. Britain also suffered indirectly since the collapse in American purchases reduced still further the earnings of those struggling primary-producing countries. They were forced to cut back on their purchases of manufactured goods, including British goods. Britain's export-oriented economy was once again punished, companies reduced their output or went out of business, and unemployment again rose, to a savage 22.1 per cent of the insured labour force in 1932. On average that year 2,828,000 insured workers were unemployed. Thereafter, paradoxically, the acute depression of the primary producers caused such a fall in the price of food and raw materials that the consequent drop in the cost of living actually helped economic recovery in Britain. The employed, who remained the great majority, found their money went further, and rising consumer spending stimulated new growth. Many of the unemployed were then re-employed. The peak of recovery came in 1937. Signs of another downturn and more unemployment appeared in 1938 only to be checked by the flurry of economic activity in the armaments, shipbuilding and iron and steel trades which preceded and then accompanied the declaration of war. Obliged to prepare for combat, the government unwittingly hit upon the cure for cyclical depression.

These cyclical downturns affected most businesses and therefore workers in most trades, though the records show that manual workers were more vulnerable than white-collar workers. High rates of unemployment were naturally recorded in the export trades. In 1932 for example, 35 per cent of coalminers and 31 per cent of cotton workers were out of work. But in addition 36 per cent of pottery workers were unemployed, 22 per cent of furniture

7

makers, 30 per cent of builders, even 17 per cent in the expanding electrical engineering and chemical industries. Moreover, most regions of the country were affected in the troughs of cyclical depression. In 1932 unemployment rates were highest in the northern areas and in Wales, ranging from 25.8 per cent to 36.5 per cent, but even in London the rate was unusually high at 13.5 per cent and in the Midlands it reached 20.1 per cent. A similar spread is apparent in the earlier downturn in 1921.

This cyclical pattern did, then, make opportunities for employment uncertain between the wars. Although a minority only were put out of work, it was an unusually large minority, and it added to the normal insecurity of working-class life. But at least victims of cyclical unemployment tended to be out of work only briefly. Grim though even temporary unemployment could be, the records show that the great majority of the unemployed were out of work for less than six months. This was not, however, true of all workers. Beneath the rapid up and down waves of cyclical unemployment lay the deep waters of structural depression into which many workers sank.

It is noticeable that even at the top of the trade cycles in 1929 and 1937, economic recovery still left an official unemployment rate of 10.4 per cent and 10.8 per cent respectively. Before the First World War and again after the Second World War, unemployment in good years was usually around 2 per cent, made up of workers briefly caught between jobs, the seasonally unemployed such as many in the building and holiday trades, and those physically and mentally handicapped and yet still endeavouring to remain in the labour force. But added to those totals between the wars went perhaps a further 8 per cent, victims of structural unemployment. They were clustered heavily in particular trades. In 1929, some 25 per cent of shipbuilders and repairers were still out of work in spite of economic recovery, 19 per cent of coalminers, 17 per cent of iron and steel workers, 13 per cent of cotton workers. There were similar high rates at the next peak in the trade cycle in 1937.

It was unfortunate that investment in these staple industries actually increased in response to wartime needs for iron and steel, ships, cloth for uniforms and coal for power and also in a misjudged expectation of a surge in demand after the war. In fact, there was a permanent decline in demand at home and especially overseas for their products. For example, world consumption of coal grew much more slowly after the First World War than before, partly because of more efficient uses of the fuel and partly because of a shift to new sources of power like oil, gas and electricity. Moreover, British coal producers found it difficult to retain their share of the international market. Competition was fiercer and more damaging, partly because of inefficiency in British production especially in the 1920s, perhaps because of the return to the gold standard in 1925 which probably left British goods over-priced in foreign markets, but most seriously because during the war more coal mines had been opened up in Germany, Poland, the Netherlands, Spain and the Far East. These rivals after the war were often protected by tariff barriers against British imports. As a result, even in the best years between the wars, British coal output was 60m. tons below the pre-war record, and fewer miners were needed to hew it. It is a similar story in the other major export industries: an increase in foreign competition, as from the new textile factories in Japan and India and from new shipyards in the United States and Scandinavia, a change in consumer demand, for example from cotton to man-made fibres and from iron to steel, and foreign protective tariffs excluding British goods. As Britain's share of international markets slumped, so did employment prospects.

One response to these adverse conditions was to shift national economic resources, including labour, out of these traditional export industries. Businessmen, aided by government, attempted to do that. The Lancashire Cotton Corporation, set up in 1929, attempted to reduce the size of the industry, and legislation in 1936 obliged the cotton trade literally to destroy surplus textile machinery. Similar schemes were begun in the coal industry and in shipbuilding in 1930, and later the iron and steel industry was given tariff protection by the National Government on the understanding that it reorganized its plant and closed excess capacity. The result of these so-called rationalization schemes in the short term was, of course, more unemployment. What was needed was to match this reduction in the size of declining industries by a transfer of resources, including labour, into the expanding building and distributive trades and the newer industries such as vehicle production, electrical engineering, chemicals and plastics. In part this happened. As already observed, the occupational structure of Britain was being transformed, and hence the great majority of the labour force stayed in employment. But it must not be imagined that this unplanned redeployment of labour was a painless operation. It constituted major surgery and there were casualties. This is revealed in those high figures for structural unemployment (6, 9).

One symptom of the problem was the appearance of long-term unemployment. In the 1920s unemployment was almost entirely short-term, but whereas in September 1929 only about 45,000 workers applying for relief had been out of work for twelve months or more, by August 1932 they numbered over 412,000 and constituted 16.4 per cent of the total out of work. Later, when overall levels of unemployment declined, the relative burden of long-term unemployment actually rose, so that the 332,000 in this category in August 1936 formed 25 per cent of the total. Not surprisingly they were largely made up of unemployed coalminers, textile workers, shipbuilders and ironworkers. There seemed little prospect of their being absorbed by other expanding trades.

In fact, several obstacles prevented a smooth transfer of labour. For one thing, the competition for jobs was bound to increase since the population continued to rise. Those of working age, 14 and over, increased in Great Britain by nearly $6\frac{1}{2}$m. between 1911 and 1931, and while not all that increase was of people actively seeking to join the labour force, the number of jobs would still have to expand simply in order to keep pace with the rising demand. Moreover, there was nothing to guarantee that those unemployed from the declining industries would have priority and would find work in trades which were expanding. Employers operated in a free market and chose the labour they thought most suitable. There was no reason to assume that an ex-miner was best qualified for employment in the car or electrical engineering industries which needed different skills. Nor, of course, was it inevitable that workers would be eager to abandon old skills and occupations and launch into something new. The change was perhaps easier for the young to make than for the old, and perhaps for that reason employers tended to recruit younger workers as fitter and more adaptable (and sometimes cheaper) than older workers. The result is apparent in the age composition of the unemployed. Unemployment and especially long-term unemployment affected youngsters least severely and became particularly severe for the middle-aged. In 1931 when the unemployment rate for men aged 25 to 44 was 13 per cent, it was 22.6 per cent for those aged 55 to 64. Structural economic change consigned many working men after half a lifetime of active labour to premature and unwelcome retirement.

The mismatch between the unemployed and new jobs was, however, even more striking in terms of geography. Most of the export industries shedding labour had been established in and around the coalfields in the North and West. Much of the new industrial investment was located in the Midlands and the South East. Indeed, between 1932 and 1937 nearly half the new factories opened in Great Britain were located in Greater London alone. Gleaming new factories around London's North Circular Road, or in Slough, Croydon and Dagenham, or in Oxford, Coventry and Bristol were of little immediate use to the unemployed miner, shipbuilder, ironfounder, cotton operative or other dispossessed worker in Co. Durham, on Tyneside, by the Clyde, on the coast of Cumberland, in South Lancashire, West Yorkshire or South Wales. Local labour, naturally growing, invariably had first pick, leaving those in the North and West with a grim future. Not surprisingly, in a boom year like 1937 the unemployment rates in London, the South East and the Midlands were around 6 or 7 per cent whereas rates elsewhere could be two or three times greater, 22.3 per cent, for example, in Wales.

Of course, the so-called distressed areas were not uniformly bleak. Pockets of new investment did occur, a little of it in the 1930s due to such government encouragement as the Special Areas Acts which among other things led to new trading estates like that at Team Valley near Gateshead. A buoyant machine-tool industry made Halifax a prosperous community in the general gloom of surrounding West Riding woollen towns. Likewise

11

new steel plants at Consett in Co. Durham and at Ebbw Vale in Monmouth brought local relief. Mixed industry towns like Manchester did not do too badly either. It was the towns and districts dependent on virtually a single industry which could be devastated without compensating fresh investment, like the shipbuilding town of Barrow-in-Furness where unemployment affected almost half the manual labour force in 1922 or the coal town of Rhondda in South Wales where in September 1936 over a quarter of the workforce had been unemployed for more than a year.

One might expect an equalization of regional unemployment rates to take place through the migration of unemployed workers in search of those new jobs elsewhere in the country. From 1928 the government encouraged such movement with modest cash assistance under an industrial transference scheme. But ties of family and community, local loyalties, misplaced hope in local economic recovery and simple inertia induced most workers to stay at home, stick it out and live on their unemployment pay. Those who did move tended to be young men and women with fewer domestic obligations and perhaps more adventurous. For many the adventure turned sour and they returned home, defeated by homesickness and a failure to find regular work. There were, after all, pools of unemployed even in towns with expanding industries, and the trickling in of unemployed aliens from outside occasionally fired the hostility which established communities sometimes show to immigrants. In Oxford, for example, there was some resentment against the intrusion of Welsh workers seeking employment in the motor industry.

Nevertheless, some migration did take place, enough to help explain the curiously unequal rates of population growth in different parts of the country. Whereas the population of London and the Home Counties increased by 18 per cent between 1921 and 1937 and the Midlands by 11 per cent, the population of Lancashire grew by less than 1 per cent, that of Northumberland and Durham actually fell by nearly 1 per cent and that of South Wales dropped by an alarming 9 per cent. Since those who moved to new jobs in new areas tended to be the young and enterprising, the effect upon the communities they left behind could be serious, socially as well as economically. Some industrial towns and villages came to contain a disproportionately ageing population and lost something of their vitality (9).

Great Britain had never been a homogeneous society, least of all in terms of employment structures. These naturally varied according to local economic activities. Between the wars, as in the past, employment history shows regional contrasts. While overall the national economy provided work for the great majority of those who sought it, even in times of cyclical depression, this blessing was distributed unevenly. But there had been a striking change. During the nineteenth century in Britain's first period of industrialization, the greater employment opportunities were to be found in the expanding industrial centres in Lancashire, Yorkshire, Co. Durham, Clydeside and South Wales, and to those areas labour had migrated. Less attractive, with the important exception of London, had been regions to the South and East. That pattern was reversed between the wars, seemingly for the indefinite future. The North and West became, and for the most part have remained, the areas with the least attractive opportunities for employment. That is one reason why the employment history of interwar Britain has such particular significance.

Family income and expenditure

As already noted, employment was the principal means by which the income of most families in Britain was acquired. The level of family income was obviously crucial to living standards, since most of the material needs of families, then as now, had to be bought: food, clothing, household equipment, other consumer goods. Houses, too, usually had to be bought or rented. Moreover, several leisure activities had to be paid for. Many services, such as health treatment, were also bought, either directly by the payment of fees or indirectly through insurance contributions. One way of assessing levels of family income in Britain is therefore to look at national expenditure on a selection of such goods and services. The figures reveal rising expenditure by the great mass of British people between the wars. This gives a strong indication that in spite of high rates of unemployment and contrary to some popular impressions of the period today, interwar Britain was for most people on balance a period of improving living standards.

Expenditure on food was naturally one of the first obligations on the family's budget. Many sources indicate increased food consumption between the wars. The quantity of food being consumed increased pretty steadily, requiring higher production by Britain's farmers and larger imports from overseas especially of meat, butter and cheese. The price of food generally fell, thus helping consumption, but even when measured in real terms, that is at the prices which were being charged by 1938, there was an almost steadily rising national expenditure on food in the United Kingdom, from £835m. in 1920 to £1,177m. in 1939. Bearing in mind that the population was also growing, it is worth noting that this still constituted a rising consumption of food per head, or per mouth, of the population. Much more of this food was being processed, packaged and distributed as branded goods by expanding food production and retail companies. Heinz, Crosse and Blackwell, Kellogg's, Sainsbury's, United Dairies and Mac Fisheries became household names (12). In spite of this increased consumption, figures show that expenditure on food was taking a much smaller slice of the budget of an average family than before the First World War. This meant that more money was available to meet other needs. Expenditure on clothing, for example, especially on mass-produced off-the-peg clothes increased. It became rare between the wars, rather than common as before 1914, to see bare-footed ragged children in the streets and at school. More will be said later about the buying or renting of the 4.3m. new houses erected in Great Britain between the wars, another indication of rising living standards. Money was also available for increased expenditure on equipment with which to stock these houses. Expenditure on furniture was rising, and novel electrical appliances became particularly common during the 1930s. Sales of vacuum cleaners doubled from 200,000 per year in 1930 to 400,000 in 1938. The sales of electric cookers trebled between 1930 and 1935. Consumer expenditure on radio equipment more than trebled between 1930 and 1938, the number of radio licenses having reached 3m. by 1929 and 9m. by the end of the 1930s. By then about three-quarters of Britain's homes could tune in to the BBC and perhaps Radio

Luxemburg. Consumer spending on such goods was, of course, tempting when so many more homes were wired up for electricity, only one house in seventeen in 1920 but two houses in every three by 1939. Also encouraging such sales was the development of the hire purchase system. Borrowing money to buy goods was an old device, even among working-class families, but rising incomes and effective advertising and salesmanship explain the huge increase in this method of tempting consumers. It was widespread for the purchase of furniture and household goods, and was also used in buying motor cars and motor cycles. Neither of these, it is true, were yet mass consumer goods, in spite of mass production techniques. A small Austin Seven selling at £118 in 1931 was still an outlay beyond virtually all working-class families, but the $\frac{1}{2}$m. vehicles on the road in 1920 had become over 3m. by 1939, almost two-thirds of these being private cars. The distinctive smell of Britain's towns ceased to be horse manure as before 1914 and became petrol exhaust, the noxious perfume of the twentieth century.

While the motor car remained still socially rather exclusive this was less true of other forms of consumer self-indulgence. While expenditure on alcoholic drink per head of the population went down by almost half between 1910–14 and 1935–38, expenditure on tobacco doubled over the same period to make the peculiar vice of cigarette smoking seemingly universal and socially acceptable (though not entirely so for women). New forms of recreation, however, increased to receive their share of disapproval from social critics. Some saw social decay in the large numbers of dance halls which sprang up in most towns, vibrating to Charleston, Black Bottom, jazz and even waltz rhythms. Equally disturbing appeared the enormous increase in popular gambling, especially the football pools through which by 1938 about 10m. people each week were buying a little hope and excitement, spending £40m. a year in the process and making firms like Littlewoods and Vernons well known, and rich. Meanwhile, greyhound racing, beginning at Belle Vue in Manchester in 1926, became another opportunity for popular gambling as well as joining established spectator sports like football as a leisure activity to be paid for and enjoyed. But it has been said, not without reason, that the interwar years and especially the 1930s were the age of the cinema. With the advent of 'talkies' in 1929, cinema attendance became obsessive. In the United Kingdom nearly 1000m. tickets a year were sold by 1938, drawing £40m. from devotees. One survey calculated that 40 per cent of the people of Liverpool went to performances once a week, and 25 per cent twice a week or more (1). Moralists might lament these practices, but for economists these further developments of the commercial leisure industry were proof that Britain was becoming a modern consumer society and that a mass market existed with substantial amounts to spend beyond immediate family needs.

Another important indication of an improvement in family income levels is the apparent decline in the extent of poverty in British society. Defining poverty is fraught with difficulties, but before the First World War social investigators like Seebohm Rowntree had established the concept of the poverty line. This defined the minimum income needed by families of different size to meet essential expenditure on rent, heating, lighting, clothing, minimum household equipment and the food required for basic nutritional needs. Families not having this minimum income were classed as living in poverty. Using this definition and employing the same standards of minimum needs as previously, social investigators repeated between the wars the examinations of urban poverty they had carried out before the First World War. The results were striking. One study of Northampton, Warrington, Reading, Stanley (in Co. Durham) and Bolton showed that even by 1923–4 the number of working-class families lacking the minimum income for subsistence had fallen by about a half over the preceding decade. Similarly, a study of London found that poverty had dropped by 1928 to about one-third of the level of 1889–91. This result is comparable to Rowntree's own study of York where he found that the 15.5 per cent of the working class in poverty in 1899 had fallen on the same standard to 6.8 per cent by 1936. These conclusions are important evidence that rising living standards were not being enjoyed just by those who by pre-1914 standards were already quite well off (8, 13).

How are we to explain such improvements in a period which in the popular memory is often equated with economic depression? The first important point to recognize is that in spite of the evidence

16

of distressed industries, occupations and areas, the country as a whole grew significantly richer. Great Britain in 1918 was already by contemporary international standards a very wealthy country, but her rate of economic growth thereafter was historically rapid. Economic growth is best expressed as the rate of annual increase in Gross Domestic Product per head, that is, in the value of all the goods and services produced at home divided by the number of people in the country. At 1913 prices, GDP per head in 1920 was, at £47, little higher than that in 1900. But the best available figures suggest an annual rate of growth of GDP per head of 1.8 per cent between 1924 and 1937. These years are chosen as showing roughly comparable points in the trade cycle whose movements naturally affected annual output. The rate may not sound very great but it raised GDP per head by 1937 to £60. Moreover, this growth rate was much faster than in the past, certainly better than in the decade before the First World War and probably better than in the Victorian period of industrial expansion when the annual rate was about 1.1 per cent from 1855 to 1900. The improvement in fact seems to be part of an acceleration towards the annual 2.3 per cent recorded in the so-called age of affluence running from 1951 to 1965.

Much of the explanation for this growth must be seen in the investment between the wars in new technology. This raised considerably the average output from the labour force. Some of these technical innovations were in what are commonly called the new industries such as chemicals, plastics, man-made fibres, electrical engineering and the manufacturing of a new range of consumer goods. The public services of gas, water and electricity also grew, the latter being a highly efficient new source of power. Building was also important although its productivity record was below average. But while these industries increased their output and as noted recruited larger labour forces to man them, improvements in productivity through new technology were also apparent in some old industries. For example, the introduction of coal-cutting machinery in the pits, of improved welding techniques in shipbuilding, of new steel-making processes, and of a few lesser innovations in the textile trade succeeded in raising the efficiency even of these well-established businesses. A great deal was also achieved by the shedding of workers from these industries which reduced over-manning and made higher demands upon the surviving labour force. For example, in the 1930s the number of looms which an individual weaver was obliged to tend was generally raised from four to six. Moreover, these old industries though declining in size were as yet still larger in terms of their total output than the newer expanding ones. Economic growth between the wars in fact owed at least as much to leaner but more efficient old industries as it did to new ones (2, 4, 6).

Economic growth, punctured as it was by cyclical depression, was by no means smooth. But over the period as a whole the economy was making society substantially richer than ever before. More goods and services were being created for the people's consumption and more income was being generated with which to purchase them. Here was an opportunity to raise living standards. That this actually happened reflects a second factor, namely that this new wealth was not monopolized by the few but was distributed to the many.

Most strikingly wage-earners enjoyed a real improvement in their levels of pay compared with the years before 1914. Much of this was due to the rapid rise in money wage levels during the First World War and in the postwar boom when the demand for labour was high. By 1920 money wages were on average nearly three times higher than before the war. Rapid rises in prices at the same time did not quite offset these increases, so that improvements in real earnings took place. This was especially true of previously very low-paid unskilled workers: differentials in pay closed significantly to bring their standard of living closer to that of skilled workers. At the same time, wage-earners as a whole gained a little on white-collar salaried workers whose earnings rose less rapidly. These relative gains were never subsequently eroded. However, with the depression following the boom and employers attacking war-inflated pay rates in the teeth of bitter trade union resistance, money wages fell fast in the early 1920s. Many were to be cut again in the depression in the early 1930s and were to rise only slowly thereafter. By 1939 money wages were only about twice the pre-First World War rates. This left the average earnings of male workers at around £3 a week, generally a little higher in newer industries and lower in the old staples, and with women at best earning about two-thirds of men's rates. Fortunately for living standards, this overall fall in money wages from the high level of 1920 was itself offset by equally rapid falls in prices. The cost of living fell almost continuously from 1920 to 1934, especially in the early 1920s and early 1930s, and rose only gradually thereafter. The net result was that average real wage earnings stayed up, and were by 1938 as much as 30 per cent higher than they had been in 1913. For those who stayed in work, and that means the majority, this was a substantial improvement (6).

Moreover, this was not the only working-class gain in these years. Holidays with pay for wage-earners had been rare before 1914, but between 1931 and 1939 the number of people entitled to paid holidays rose from 1½m. to 11m. Amongst other things this explains the increased popularity of annual holidays by the sea, attracting 20m. people a year in the late 1930s. One other gain achieved earlier in 1919–20 had been a general reduction in the standard working hours from around 54 a week before the war to around 48. This reduction increased the opportunity either for greater overtime earnings or for more leisure activities. In either case it marked an improvement in living standards. It is true that working people and especially the poor suffered disproportionately between the wars from relatively high tax burdens, especially from duties on tea, sugar, tobacco and alcohol, but even these burdens did not eliminate the considerable financial gains which the employed working class as a whole experienced.

It is, however, as well to remember that they were not the only beneficiaries from the rise in money incomes in the war and in the boom and from the fall in prices thereafter. In many respects inter-war Britain was a golden age for middle-class, white-collar salary-earners. It is true that the very wealthy took a slightly less large share of national income and found their tax burden had grown quite markedly with the war. But for those earning between £250 and £1000 a year, the loss of income to the taxman had increased little since before the First World War. We should remember that the expansion in the number of white-collar occupations did, of course, involve recruiting children from working-class families. Their new jobs were usually more secure, their working conditions were better and they were blessed by rising real incomes. Most middle-class consumers found much to enjoy between the wars. It was then possible to motor on relatively quiet roads. Holidays by the sea away from the major resorts remained peaceful and rather exclusive. More families ventured abroad. While having a resident domestic servant was no longer as before the First World War the necessary badge of middle-class respectability, middle-class homes managed quite nicely with the new labour-saving vacuum cleaners, gas and electric cookers, refrigerators and Ascot water-heaters. Besides, it was usually quite easy and cheap to find a 'little woman' to pop in as a daily help and do the cleaning.

One other remarkable development helps explain the rising living standards of the occupied population. Middle-class couples had started limiting the size of their families from about the 1880s and this trend towards fewer children becomes increasingly apparent and included more working-class parents between the wars. The birth rate in England and Wales had been 26.3 per 1000 of the population in 1906–10 (slightly higher in Scotland) and fell to 14.7 per 1000 by 1936–40 (still higher at 17.6 per 1000 in Scotland). This resulted in a significant fall in the number of children per marriage. Women married in 1910 had on average three children, and of 1000 women marrying in that year 200 had between five and nine children. Those married in 1930 had on average only 2.1 children and only 100 out of a 1000 had such large families. This reduction in the birth rate, as much as anything, marked a real emancipation for women. It is known that contraception explains this fall in fertility. Something is also known about the propaganda for the use of particular contraceptive methods: Dr Marie Stopes opened her first birth control clinic in 1920. But the reasons why parents wished at this time to limit the size of their families are complex and less than clear (2). The effects on living standards are, however, striking and important. Even by 1924 one investigation of working-class families concluded that 'this diminution in the number of children has had a marked effect on the proportion found in poverty'. Obviously, with fewer mouths to feed and bodies to clothe, family income went further. Cash was increasingly left over for other purchases. As A. J. P. Taylor put it, with reference to middle-class families: 'The baby Austin ousted the baby. The nursery gave place to the garage'.

A combination of economic and demographic factors was therefore responsible for the observable increase in average family incomes and expenditure between the wars. Nevertheless, we cannot ignore that this was a society in which poverty remained endemic. All contemporary social investigators recognized that in spite of the progress recorded significantly large numbers of people still fell below their poverty lines. It is true that the level of the poverty line was raised, mainly to incorporate new knowledge about nutritional needs in calculating the cost of minimum diets. But Rowntree also included a minimum expenditure on beer, tobacco, a wireless, newspapers and other personal items in his 1936 definition of the poverty line, and this meant that his poverty line was raised as social expectations of a proper living standard rose. Inequalities in society were vividly revealed. Rowntree found that by his new definition 31.1 per cent of the working-class population of York lived in poverty in 1936. Other investigators adopted different standards and examined different towns in different years, but they too found, for example, that 17.3 per cent of working-class families on Merseyside lived in poverty in 1929–30, 20 per cent in Southampton in 1931, and 10.7 per cent even in prosperous Bristol in 1936.

The causes of poverty were the same as before the First World War, but their comparative virulence had altered. Low wages were still a major cause of poverty, the largest single cause in York, but the depth of poverty which resulted had declined. This reflected those improvements already noted in the pay especially of the unskilled. The sickness or death of the breadwinner still caused substantial amounts of deep financial distress, a reflection in part of the low levels of relief granted by state health insurance and widows' pensions schemes. Of growing concern was the deep poverty of the elderly, especially of those dependent on inadequate state old age pensions: life expectancy was increasing so that more people were surviving into retirement age only to peter out in poverty. The poverty due to unemployment was also deep and had increased: while a few unemployed people living on unemployment relief found themselves no worse off on the dole than

21

if they had been working in their previous low-paid jobs, this was not true of the majority. Unemployment assistance was between 45 and 66 per cent of average former wages, varying according to age. At least the unemployed were guaranteed relief equivalent to the pay of most employed unskilled labourers before the First World War. Since that had normally involved living in poverty this was little consolation. The family with dependent children would find it especially hard to remain above the poverty line.

Children remained in fact a major cause of poverty, in spite of the decline in the birth rate. Working-class families were still on average larger than those of the middle classes. Before the Second World War there were no child benefit or family allowances, and therefore wages alone had to support most working-class families. This burden explains Rowntree's discovery that over *half* the working-class children born in York in 1936 were born into poverty. This was the first stage in the poverty cycle he identified. Most of the children born into poverty would rise above it when they or their siblings became wage-earners, only to sink below it in many cases when they became parents themselves. Over a quarter of working-class people in York aged between 25 and 44 were in poverty. For some, relief would come when their children became wage-earners in turn. Comparative prosperity was then arrested for many of those who survived into old age since nearly half of those aged over 65 fell below the poverty line (8, 13). Not surprisingly, traditional working-class strategies for survival in the face of insecurity and poverty remained in operation between the wars: the use of the pawnbroker, 'tick' or credit at the corner shop, knowledge of the cheapest sources of food, and above all the mutual support of neighbours. It was practice in these arts which enabled working-class communities to survive the new burden of severe cyclical and structural unemployment (15).

Naturally it followed that living standards and the extent and depth of poverty varied geographically, broadly as a reflection of local economic conditions. Information on regional income levels is rather thin, but since unemployment was a major cause of poverty it was inevitable that poverty was greater in the depressed areas than elsewhere. The physical appearance of particularly hard-hit towns was one sign of this: observers noted the signs of disrepair, of broken windows, of peeling paint and the number of shops closed down and boarded up for lack of business when local purchasing power fell. J. B. Priestley in *English Journey* (1934) reckoned that one out of every two shops in shipwrecked Jarrow was closed. Inevitably too, local pools of unemployment drove down local wage levels and increased another cause of poverty. One estimate of 1934 suggests that nearly 80 per cent of chief income earners in South Wales earned less than £4 a week compared with only 68 per cent in London and the South East. While the prevalence of poverty and the inequalities in income were not new features of British society, this reduction of the North and West to a low income area was, like the change in employment prospects it reflects, a reversal of nineteenth-century patterns. It must rank as another important qualification to the otherwise real record of improvements in living standards in interwar Britain.

Housing

One sign of the rising living standards of the majority of British families was the impressive amount of house-building between the wars. For one thing it demonstrated the wealth of the United Kingdom that this society could afford to invest nearly £2500m. in houses between 1920 and 1938. Such investment did indeed help the economic growth of the country and certainly the recovery during the 1930s. About 4.3m. houses were built in Great Britain between the wars, roughly 1½m. in the 1920s and 2½m. in the 1930s. Construction at this rate was historically extremely rapid. By 1939 about one family in three was living in a modern post-war house (2).

Again roughly speaking, 2½m. of these houses were built by private enterprise. This, of course, was the traditional method of housing construction, for private builders to sense and to meet public demand. Rising real incomes between the wars increased that demand while at the same time the fall in the prices of raw materials and labour actually reduced markedly the cost of houses from an immediate postwar peak. Houses similar to those costing just under £1000 in 1920 could be bought for as little as £400 later in the 1920s and in the 1930s. Encouraging the purchase of houses in the 1930s was the extraordinary ease of obtaining mortgages. Building societies were attracting an increasingly large amount of people's savings between the wars, and they were lending money in the 1930s, after the fall in the bank rate, at interest rates as low as $4\frac{1}{2}$ per cent. As a result, the number of borrowers in England and Wales increased from 554,000 in 1928 to 1,392,000 by 1937. So anxious were builders and building societies to find house purchasers that the initial deposits on houses were also reduced in the 1930s from about 25 per cent of the price to a mere 5 per cent, perhaps as little as £25. Indeed, some builders went further and even laid out the garden or offered free refrigerators, cookers and electric clocks as baits to catch purchasers. Every attempt was made through vigorous advertising to entice customers, for example, to

'Live in Ruislip where the air's like wine,
    It's less than half an hour on the Piccadilly Line.'

One clear indication of their success is shown in the rise in the number of owner-occupiers from a mere 10 per cent of families in Great Britain in 1914 to 31 per cent by 1939. Before the First World War even most middle-class families had lived in rented property, but this was no longer to be the case (10, 11).

Remarkable as that change was, it must share the limelight with a revolution in the rented property market. In 1914 only 1 per cent of families in Great Britain, mainly in London, rented council houses. By 1939 they constituted 14 per cent. This marks the astonishing entry of local authorities into the house-building business. The Addison Housing Act of 1919 gave local authorities financial subsidies from the central government and required them to build houses for let to working-class families. Though the act was abolished in 1921, this principle, with altered financial arrangements, was perpetuated by the Chamberlain Housing Act of 1923, the Wheatley Housing Act of 1924 and by the acts of 1930, 1933 and 1935 designed to cope with slum clearance and overcrowding. Private builders were also encouraged by subsidies to build houses to let, particularly under the Chamberlain Act. Altogether these central government subsidies cost the taxpayer over £208m. between 1919 and 1939 for the construction in

England and Wales of 1,112,505 council houses and 430,327 additional private houses. Scottish legislation produced 212,866 council houses and 43,067 subsidized private houses. The result of this activity was to reduce still further the comparative size of the private rented house market, and to make the council tenant a conspicuous part of the social scene for the first time.

It is not just the quantity of interwar housing which impresses: it is also, for the most part, its quality. Even many middle-class families before the First World War had lived in accommodation which to modern eyes would feel dark, cold and lacking in proper facilities. Working-class houses, even when their construction was regulated with by-laws as most were after the Public Health Act of 1875, tended to consist of grim rows of terraces. Even the best had kitchens and sculleries tacked on the back making the rear dark and often damp. High densities of as many as 40 or 50 houses to the acre had been commonplace. Earlier housing, much of which survived into the interwar period, could be a good deal worse, consisting of back-to-back houses, blind backs (with no rear windows or doors) and cellar dwellings, often grouped around gloomy courts with shared water taps and midden privies as their limited and offensive sanitary facilities. By contrast, some of the new interwar housing consisted of good quality flats in inner city areas. These were usually five or six storeys, not the skyscrapers of the present day, and they were rich with such innovations as gas fires and water heaters, baths and balconies, and sometimes they had recreation rooms, nursery facilities and communal laundries. Flats, however, made up only 5 per cent of all state-subsidized building in England and Wales between the wars, though 40 per cent in London and 20 per cent in Liverpool, and were mainly an innovation of the later 1930s. For the most part, new housing, private and municipal, consisted of semi-detached houses or short terraces of four or six houses, with a few detached houses for the better off. The appearance of these houses and estates owed a great deal to the pre-1914 designs advocated by Garden City enthusiasts like Ebenezer Howard, and to the inspiring examples of estates built particularly for philanthropic employers since the late 1880s at Port Sunlight, Bournville and New Earswick. These designs were on the whole imitated by private builders between the wars and were endorsed by the Ministry of Health for the guidance of local authorities in their construction of council houses. The design, quality of material and fittings were on average perhaps inevitably superior in private houses (though bitter attacks on the jerry-built, ramshackle products of some private building firms are not rare), but council houses also contained luxuries comparatively rare in working-class homes before 1914. They boasted gas or increasingly electric lighting, hot and cold running water, a cooker, a bath (contrary to malicious rumour, not frequently used for storing coal), and the single greatest contribution to human happiness, the indoor lavatory. There was also space, usually three bedrooms upstairs, a kitchen, and either a large living room downstairs, or a separate dining room and parlour. Houses were built at low density, rarely more than 12 to the acre, often less in private estates.

One inevitable result of such low densities was the construction by private builders and municipal authorities of estates of new property covering huge areas. During the nineteenth century, urban development had witnessed the ringing round of the major cities by suburbs. This phenomenon became even more geographically apparent as large numbers of people moved into new low density estates around the perimeters of existing urban areas. For example, between 1921 and 1934 the London County Council built at Becontree on former farmland beyond its previous frontiers what at that time was the largest planned residential suburb in the world with accommodation for 90,000 people. Manchester Corporation similarly began the construction of a vast low density estate at Wythenshawe, and a series of large council estates was laid down by the Liverpool authorities as at Norris Green. Private builders were equally responsible for the suburban spread around the cities, for example into Edgware, Morden, Rayners Lane and other districts served by London's trams, buses and Metropolitan railway systems. The name *Metroland* was coined as early as 1914 to describe the new suburbs. It was celebrated in a vocal one-step 'My Little Metro-land Home' in 1920, but it made its major social impression over subsequent years. Between 1921 and 1937 about 1.4m. people moved to outer London, enough to reduce the population of the central area by 400,000 (10, 11).

26

The new houses made possible new recreational patterns. Homes, especially working-class homes, had formerly often been rather cramped, and much leisure time had been spent in the street, by children, and in the pub, by men. Such patterns of behaviour were affected by new opportunities. Most new houses had gardens to front and back, and gardening as a popular pastime reached a scale previously unknown. Rowntree was to comment on the council estates in York:

> Every house has a front and back garden usually of some 200 to 300 square yards. In summer they are ablaze with colour. It is indeed amazing how soon families, most of whom had never had a garden before, turn the rough land surrounding their new houses into beautiful gardens.

If the country was becoming a nation of gardeners, other opportunities were available indoors, confirming the greater home-centredness of many people's lives. Increasing amounts of surplus income coupled with space indoors explains the craze for domestic hobbies between the wars. It is an interesting conjunction of social developments which led to such interwar obsessions as do-it-yourself homemaking, model-railway building and radio construction (and listening). Such opportunities and the facilities in the new housing readily explain why one council tenant reported that their new house 'was just like a palace'. An enquiry conducted just before the outbreak of the Second World War found that 80 per cent of a sample of residents in new working-class housing estates, the vast majority, were satisfied with their homes.

In the light of these considerable interwar achievements it is unfortunate that we must next record that such improvements had by no means eliminated the nation's housing problems. Complete satisfaction was perhaps unattainable since the higher quality of new housing tended to stimulate a rise in expectations, expressed as a growing dissatisfaction with much of the surviving pre-First World War and especially pre-1880 property. Estimates of the number of slum houses in the country tended to rise faster than slum houses could be torn down, or fell down. In 1934 local authorities reckoned that 333,268 houses in Great Britain were ripe for demolition. Revised programmes in 1937–9 suggested a total of 604,417. There were, however, even some criticisms of the new housing estates. It had become alarmingly apparent by the end of the 1930s that two decades of rapid suburban development had eaten hungrily into surrounding rural areas and sent out fingers of ribbon development along main roads. Urban improvement had exacerbated the problem of urban sprawl. This was to exercise the minds of town planners and politicians over succeeding decades. Furthermore, the new housing appeared to divide people into pretty strict social categories, with some apparently severe boundaries between working-class and middle-class areas. Council estates, to some observers, felt like working-class ghettoes. The Town Planning Act of 1932 seemed to encourage this division by requiring authorities to designate areas for different densities of housing, from one to twelve houses to the acre, a policy of zoning which would be socially divisive. Nevertheless, except in the remarkable case at Cutteslowe in Oxford where middle-class residents of a private estate were divided from their neighbours in the adjoining council estate by the construction in 1934 of 7 ft high, spike-topped brick walls built across the connecting roads, such social distinctions seem to have caused little explicit resentment. Council tenants complained rather more about the lack in many estates of such customary social facilities as local shops and local pubs. The latter were, for example, explicitly banned from the Norris Green estate outside Liverpool. Their absence was indicative of the departure from and the break-up of some old-established working-class communities and life styles which some residents found impossible to accept. Several families found the new estates bleak and hostile and returned to the inner city areas. It is reported that one early inhabitant of the London County Council estate at Watling roused her neighbour in alarm to ask 'What has happened? Everything is so terribly quiet'.

These problems appear minor, however, compared to the probability that even at the end of this period of vigorous house-building there remained a housing shortage. Some earlier calculations reckoned that interwar housing supply met the demand, but more recently a less optimstic conclusion has been reached. This despondent note is difficult to accept unless it is first realised that there was after the war a substantial initial housing shortage: in 1921 the number of families in the United Kingdom exceeded the number of houses by about 865,000. Secondly, from the total number of new dwellings we must subtract the number demolished. And, thirdly, we have to recognize the astonishing increase between the wars in the number of families in the country. Although the total population was increasing more slowly as family sizes shrank, the number of separate family units was actually growing quickly: indeed, the number of families in the United Kingdom increased by 3,515,000 between 1921 and 1938 which was rather more than the increase in the population as a whole! Assuming, legitimately, that families wanted homes of their own, house-builders would have to run fast simply to stand still. Although historians disagree, it is likely that at the end of this period demand for houses still exceeded supply by about 800,000.

There is, it is true, evidence of houses remaining unoccupied between the wars, 123,000 in the United Kingdom in 1920 rising to 363,000 by 1938. This is, however, perfectly compatible with a housing shortage. One explanation is that most of the houses built between the wars were beyond the financial reach of many families in need of new homes. Analysis of new housing in England and Wales shows that expensive houses, rated above £26 a year, increased by 65 per cent between 1919 and 1939, those in the £14–£26 bracket by 96 per cent and those at the bottom of the market, where the ill-housed majority lived, by only 29 per cent. An unoccupied detached house in leafy Carshalton was of no great significance to the slum dweller in Wapping. It is abundantly clear that most of the housing provided by private builders was occupied by white-collar workers and only by unusually affluent manual workers. Rowntree analysed the occupants of the 4330 post-war semi-detached houses built in York between 1920 and 1939 and found the occupants of less than one in six had an income below £250 a year, his maximum figure for defining a working-class family. Post-war private semis housed less than 4 per cent of the town's working class. The deterrent was, of course, the rent charges of almost 16s (80p) a week or, for owner-occupiers, the still higher costs of rates and mortgage repayments. Cheap though mortgages appear, they were still too dear for most working-class families.

It was the explicit intention of the council house-building programmes to provide good accommodation for working people. However, council tenants bunched along a fairly narrow social band. Analysis of tenants on five large London County Council estates showed that the majority were clerks, tradesmen, skilled workers and better-off semi-skilled workers. Comparatively few unskilled workers could afford the rent levels charged. In York rents ranged from 8s (40p) to 13s (65p) a week. Government subsidies were insufficient to enable local authorities to set them any lower. Most of the poor families who occupied council housing in York and elsewhere had been rehoused during slum clearance schemes in the 1930s, and for them rent rebate schemes might be in operation. However, by 1938 only 112 out of about 1500 housing authorities operated rent rebate schemes. Besides, council house tenants, even if they could afford the rent, found other hidden costs. For example, shopping was often more expensive in the outer suburbs than in the more competitive inner cities so that the cost of feeding a family could be greater. Then there were additional transport costs, especially for the many workers who now had to travel greater distances to work. Moreover, the larger spacious houses were usually more expensive to heat, and there are cases of rehoused families continuing to sleep in one bedroom in order to keep warm. On Liverpool estates in 1931–2, 29 per cent of tenants were in arrears with rent. Many families flitted back to cheaper property in the inner cities. Financial hardship explains why the 9.30 a.m. bus on Monday mornings from the Becontree council estate to Barking picked up passengers carrying large bundles and was known as the 'pawnshop bus' (10).

These financial problems help explain why poorer families continued to live in slum property and often in overcrowded conditions. The rents for slum houses in York in 1936 could be as little as 5s (25p) a week, and this was all that many families could afford. Even so, Rowntree found that the poorer families were still spending a substantially higher proportion of their income on rent than better-off families in superior accommodation. In 1935 the government defined overcrowding as more than three persons

30

living in a two-roomed house, five in a three-roomed house and so on up a sliding scale: using this definition Rowntree found that over half the families living in overcrowded accommodation in York did so because they could afford nothing better (13). We should also note that little direct attention was given to the demolition of and the replacement of overcrowded slum housing until after the Housing Acts of 1933 and 1935 came slowly into operation. Until then, large numbers of British people continued to occupy what only a statistician could describe as houses. By the government's own spartan standards in 1936 nearly 350,000 houses were overcrowded, and an irrecoverable additional number were damp, insanitary and alive with unwelcome wild life. 'It was in Plymouth', wrote Howard Marshall in his book *Slum* (1933),

> that in the first room I visited − it was the basement of a tall, early Victorian house − a boy had been killed by a rat. . . . The boy had been playing with his small brother on the bed . . . when the rat dropped down through a hole in the ceiling, and bit the terrified boy on the side of the face. The boy was taken to hospital, but the wound turned septic and he died.

While slum clearance work had demolished 342,940 houses in Great Britain by 1939, it is salutary to remember that in 1943, after this age of improvement, some 40 per cent of houses in Hull and 90 per cent of those in Stepney were without baths, and that 12 per cent of Birmingham's houses in 1946 had no separate lavatories. It had been assumed by government and some social observers at the time that building houses for the fairly well off would benefit all, as those at the bottom would take over the better accommodation of those who had moved to the new houses. While this must have happened quite extensively, we should not forget the financial obstacles which prevented many families from benefiting from this process of 'filtering-up'.

Finally, we should note that these problems of poor housing were distributed unequally around the country. One legacy of the nineteenth century was the huge densities of early and mid-nineteenth-century housing in inner London and the industrial towns of the Midlands, the North of England, South Wales and southern Scotland. Many of these houses were decaying fast. In

31

any case they had never been endowed with the facilities which modern expectations demanded. The deceleration in the rate of growth of population in the North and West reduced some of the pressure on housing, and comparative affluence in the Greater London area enabled private builders to meet some of the demand from the swelling numbers in that region. But the extent of remaining local problems was revealed by the surveys of 1934 which counted the number of slum houses to be demolished. They traced out the record of past industrial activity: 33,000 in London, 30,000 in Leeds, 15,000 in Manchester, nearly 12,000 in Liverpool, 9,000 in Sheffield, 4500 in Birmingham. Similarly, the overcrowding survey of 1936 showed large numbers of families living in overcrowded conditions in inner London and in many of the old industrial areas in the North: 17.2 per cent of families in Shoreditch, 20.6 per cent in Sunderland (or one family in every five). Even the 7.4 per cent in Liverpool was almost double the national average for England and Wales. The rate for Scotland was even more appalling at 22.6 per cent. By contrast, the rate in Oxford was a mere 1 per cent, in Croydon 0.9 per cent, in Bournemouth 0.3 per cent. Some ironing out of regional contrasts had been achieved by 1939, but neither this nor the other problems mentioned had been finally solved before Adolf Hitler's *Luftwaffe* set about some unselective demolition work and exacerbated the housing difficulties of Great Britain.

Health

One of the best indicators of social conditions is the health of the people. In the later nineteenth century and increasingly in the twentieth century, contemporary commentators used the records of the nation's health not only as a guide to the efficacy of welfare services but also as a social barometer measuring the consequences of ups and downs in the national and local economies, levels of unemployment and wages, the quality of housing and other environmental conditions. Such was the practice between the wars.

The Ministry of Health was first established in Britain in 1919 on the foundations principally of the former Local Government Board.

Between the wars it tended to adopt year by year a complacent tone in its annual review of the state of the nation's health. Grounds for satisfaction seem apparent: without doubt health was in general better in 1939 than twenty years earlier. Direct evidence of the population's health is actually rather limited. Mostly we have information about its opposite, sickness and especially death. What the figures show seems a story of improvement. It is true that maternal mortality rates increased rather alarmingly in England and Wales from 3.9 deaths of mothers per 1000 live births in 1921–5 to 4.3 in 1931–5, but the rate was down to 3.26 by 1937. General mortality rates had been falling since the 1870s. They averaged 14.7 per 1000 of the population in 1906–10 but only 12.0 per 1000 by 1936–8. Rowntree noted a drop in York from 17.2 deaths per 1000 in 1898–1901 to 11.6 per 1000 by 1936–8. Even more strikingly he showed that the infant mortality rate, that is the deaths of children under age one per 1000 live births, had fallen from an appalling 160.6 to 54.6 over the same period. This too was part of a national trend. The figure for England and Wales had started to fall at the turn of the century, it was 105 per 1000 in 1910, and then it dropped sharply to 60 in 1930 and less sharply to 56 in 1940. The major killer diseases of the nineteenth century like scarlet fever, diphtheria, whooping cough, measles, typhoid and tuberculosis seemed to be rapidly in retreat. To speak cheerily, we all die of some complaint in the end, but it was actually a sign of progress that death rates from the degenerative diseases of middle and old age, especially cancer and heart disease, started to take a larger toll as the virulent infectious diseases of the past wilted. A further indication of improvement was an increase in life expectancy at birth which for those born in 1901–12 had been 51.5 years for men and 55.4 for women, but for those born in 1930–32 it was 58.7 and 62.9 respectively. There are a few other clues about better health. Since we can rightly assume that genetically the British people had not changed in the interim, it was indicative of better health when Rowntree found that working-class children in York were growing a couple of inches taller on average by 1936 than in 1899 and they were about five pounds heavier. One result of this improvement was apparent when men were conscripted into the armed forces in the

Second World War: some 70 per cent were found to be fully fit. This may be compared with the mere 36 per cent recorded as fully fit when conscripted in 1917–18 (1, 7, 13).

How can we explain this record of national betterment? Not surprisingly and not unreasonably, the Ministry of Health tended to explain it in terms of improvements in the protective and curative health services for which it was responsible and in terms of the developing expertise of the medical profession. Firstly, there were further extensions in what we would now call environmental health services. These had been growing since that mid-nineteenth century attack on the urban conditions which seemed to cause the spread of infectious diseases. Central and local authorities attacked the diseases spread by the micro-organisms carried in water, food and air. Legislation was passed to improve water supplies, sanitation and working conditions, to deter food adulteration, and to improve the quality of housing. Between the wars local authorities as a rule continued to extend their controls, and they were later helped by major new laws consolidating earlier legislation: the Public Health Act of 1936, the Factory Act of 1937 and the Food and Drugs Act of 1938. In this context, most important was the improvement in housing conditions already described. The connection between slum houses, overcrowding and the spread of infectious diseases had been clearly established before the First World War. One investigation in Birmingham in 1912–16 compared an area of poor housing with an area with fairly good accommodation and revealed an infant mortality rate of 171 per 1000 live births in the former and of 89 in the latter. The beneficial effects of interwar re-housing were noted by some observers. One report, *Working-Class Wives* (1939), cited the case of Mrs W. of Brighton who had 'recently moved into a new Corporation housing estate, and has four rooms and a scullery. She says she is in much better health since she moved'.

The Ministry of Health also placed emphasis on the expansion and improvement of the medical services. National Health Insurance, introduced by law in 1911, had its weaknesses but it did cover 19m. wage-earners by 1936 and allowed them a small cash benefit when sick and off work and enabled them to consult a doctor and obtain basic treatment without charge. There were

34

also more doctors to consult: 6.2 per 10,000 of the population in 1911 growing to 7.5 per 10,000 by 1941. The number of nurses and health visitors also grew at a comparable if unspectacular rate. There were also more hospitals and hospital beds: 5.48 beds per 1000 of the population in 1911, 6.41 by 1938. The Maternity and Child Welfare Act of 1918 encouraged local authorities to establish welfare clinics and the number of expectant and nursing mothers using the service grew. By 1936 over 60 per cent of children born in England and over 69 per cent of children born in Wales were brought to the 3368 infant welfare centres run by local authorities and voluntary bodies. As for children at school, the system of medical inspection and treatment set up before the First World War continued to operate and slightly expanded to include the greater provision of school meals and later of school milk. It should also be noted that on the whole medical expertise improved: particularly important was the development and availability after 1935 of a range of life-saving sulphonamide drugs, used for example in the treatment of pneumonia, measles and scarlet fever.

Some contemporary commentators were not satisfied, however, that health improvements were solely or even primarily the product of better environmental conditions and advances in medicine and health services. For example, Dr M'Gonigle, the Medical Officer of Health for Stockton-on-Tees, claimed in a much quoted book, *Poverty and Public Health* (1936), that 'environment is not the only factor . . . and possibly not the most important one'. Historians have tended to agree. Between the wars more emphasis was placed on the crucial link between nutrition and health. It was understood by the end of the nineteenth century that the body operated basically like a machine and needed, roughly speaking, fuel for energy, from carbohydrates, fats and protein, but also further protein for body-building and repairs. However, in the decades before and after the First World War much more knowledge was gained about other crucial dietetic needs, for vitamins and minerals. These, it was discovered, were vital in protecting the body from disease. Their absence led to anaemia, defective eyes, teeth and bones and other illnesses. Severe deficiency caused rickets, and since this could, amongst other things, cause a deformed pelvis it increased the risks of child-birth for mother and child. Moreover, poor diet left the body unable to fight off tuberculosis and other infectious diseases. The healthy body was not one which simply avoided contamination by germs, but a body which manufactured the natural antibodies to defeat infection. The importance of adequate diet in this task was suggested by the condition of troops in the trenches on the Western Front who, if not shot by the enemy, remained in remarkably good health on proper army rations in spite of appalling environmental circumstances. Dr M'Gonigle also conducted a famous study to monitor the effects of moving half the residents of a slum area in Stockton into a bright new modern council estate. In spite of this superior environment the death rate on the council estate was actually higher than among the residents left in the other half of the slum. The explanation was that the relatively higher rents on the council estates obliged the tenants to cut back their spending on food. The poorer quality of their diet left them more vulnerable to disease and death. These discoveries gave a new meaning to the word malnutrition. For the pioneers in dietetic research, it no longer meant starvation or even feelings of hunger: it meant the failure to eat a diet incorporating all the ingredients necessary for perfect health.

It may now be seen that another explanation for the overall improvement in the nation's health offered itself. The increased amounts of food consumed per head of the population has already been mentioned as evidence of a rise in living standards. It is now time to look more closely at what kind of food was consumed in greater quantities. This shows a marked improvement overall in the quality of the nation's diet. In 1936 Sir John Boyd Orr published figures in his controversial report *Food, Health and Income*. He showed that the consumption of potatoes in 1934 per head of the population had scarcely altered since before the First World War, and the consumption of wheat flour, mainly in the form of bread, had actually decreased slightly: these were the traditional energy-giving hunger-suppressing foods of poor people in Western societies. Consumption of meat on the other hand had risen slightly since 1909–13, while that of butter, eggs and cheese had risen by about 50 per cent. Consumption of fresh vegetables other than potatoes had risen by 64 per cent and of such fruit as apples, oranges and bananas by as much as 88 per cent. As Orr commented, these were 'increases in foods of high biological value . . . they represent an increased intake of essential vitamins and mineral salts'. The result was a falling death rate, taller children, increased life expectancy. 'Accompanying that improvement in diet, there has been a corresponding improvement in national health' (8, 12). It followed, of course, that the way to improve the nation's health still further was to encourage more widely the consumption of good diets. The Ministry of Health did, indeed, set out to educate the public in the new dietetic knowledge, instructing mothers at welfare clinics on the appropriate diets for themselves and their children, and ensuring with the co-operation of the Board of Education that domestic science acquired a prominent place on the school curriculum for girls, the wives and mothers of the future. There was an official belief too that better nutritional knowledge, plus further improvements in medical services, would also reduce the high maternal mortality rate, a particularly worrying and stubborn feature of the nation's health record in the middle of the period.

Impressive as the overall improvement in the nation's health may seem to be, critics at the time and since have rightly drawn attention to the dark seam which underlines this story and which the official records tended to ignore. National health statistics were mainly expressed in terms of national averages. But such averages disguised some significant discrepancies. There were, for example, wide differences in levels of health according to people's social class. In most respects the higher up the social scale a family was, the better was the health of its members. The death rate for men aged 20 to 64 in higher professional or similar occupations in 1930–32 was 10 per cent below the standardized rate for England and Wales as a whole but for unskilled labourers it was 11 per cent above the rate. For the first group of men, deaths from tuberculosis in 1930–32 were 39 per cent below the standard and for the second group they were 25 per cent above. It was a wise child that got itself born to a professional middle-class father in 1930–32: the infant mortality rate in that class was 33 per 1000 legitimate live births, compared with 77 per 1000 in unskilled workers' homes (7).

It is doubtful whether these social discrepancies were due to genetic differences, though some people at the time claimed this to be the case. It seems much more likely that it was due to inequalities in income. Rowntree, for example, in his survey of York in 1936 divided the working class into five groups according to the level of family income: in the top two groups, both above his poverty line, the death rate was 8.4 per 1000 of the population, but for the bottom two groups, below the poverty line, it was 13.5. Similarly with infant mortality rates in York, the contrast was between 41.3 deaths per 1000 live births for the better-off families and 77.7 deaths for the poorer. Rowntree also demonstrated that children from the better-off homes grew taller and heavier than those from poorer homes (13).

There are several reasons why health was likely to vary according to family income. Before the establishment of the National Health Service after the Second World War, welfare services were at best rudimentary in structure and cover. The medical care people received depended a good deal on how much they could afford to pay. For example, while most wage-earners were covered by the National Health Insurance scheme, neither dependent wives nor children were, and for them either separate private insurance cover had to be taken out or medical expenses had to be paid for in cash. Poor people, unable to afford treatment, often did not seek medical advice. The report on *Working-Class Wives* showed that many women either could not afford to consult a doctor or could not afford the treatment recommended.

Moreover, it will be realized from what has already been said about housing, that the poorest people tended inevitably to live in slums and overcrowded conditions, and they were therefore the more vulnerable to infectious diseases. Dr Addison, the first Minister of Health, recorded in the book he wrote after leaving office, *The Betrayal of the Slums* (1922), that in one London borough only 86 out of 482 tuberculosis patients coming to a local dispensary had a bedroom to themselves: nearly all the rest had to share not only a room but even a bed with someone else, thus increasing the risk of spreading infection. In another investigation in 1933, the Medical Office of Health for Birmingham analysed infant mortality in the city and contrasted the rate of 59 deaths per 1000 live births in the newer outer ring of suburbs with the 89 deaths per 1000 live births in the central wards where most slum houses remained (8).

However, the new understanding of the dietetic basis of health provided contemporaries with another explanation of social inequalities in health. Different social groups had different records of health because their different levels of family income enabled the richer to eat more expensive and more balanced diets and the poorer were obliged to eat cheaper and less nutritious meals. Vulnerability to disease accordingly differed. This conclusion was demonstrated by a number of investigators. Sir John Boyd Orr's study was the most provocative since his work helped to explain not only the irrefutable evidence of health improvements but also the inequalities in health between classes. The method he and his co-workers in the field adopted was to collect information about the amount and type of food actually consumed by families in different income groups around the country. He then analysed these diets in order to see how far they contained the ingredients he believed necessary for perfect health. His results were alarming. Firstly, the amount of money spent on food fell the poorer families were. Secondly, the consumption of important foodstuffs like milk, butter, cheese, fish, eggs, fruit, green vegetables and meat also fell as poverty increased. Thirdly, and as a consequence, the consumption of calories, carbohydrates, proteins, fats, minerals and vitamins was also reduced the lower the family income was. Indeed, only the wealthiest of his groups actually had an intake of *all* the ingredients he believed essential. He concluded that in general 'a diet completely adequate for health according to modern standards is reached only at an income level above that of 50 per cent of the population' (8, 12).

This conclusion aroused considerable debate, but other studies supported the broadly similar conclusion that malnutrition, as redefined, was far from uncommon in modern Britain and was particularly apparent among lower income groups. While ignorance about food values and unwise expenditure of family income in other directions partly explained poor diets, it is clear that this was not the substantial explanation. Dr M'Gonigle and others showed that though the poor spent less in cash terms on food, they actually spent more as a proportion of family income than wealthier groups. Their choice of foodstuffs was also on the whole the most sensible they could manage. Rowntree concluded from his own study of malnutrition in York, 'it can only be remedied by increasing the income of the families concerned or lowering the cost of food'.

The links between income, nutrition and health also explain the evidence that at least in the worst years of the economic depression the pace of health improvements was checked or even reversed. Unemployment and cuts in wages did not immediately doom large numbers to an early grave as their incomes fell, but there are strong hints that the families of the unemployed could neverthe-less be seriously affected. Studies showed that the consumption of meat, vegetables, fruit and milk was usually proportionately lower in unemployed families than among the employed. More-over, there was evidence that the health of unemployed workers was generally worse than that of employed workers. M'Gonigle in Stockton-on-Tees compared families of the unemployed with those of the employed and discovered that though similar in most other respects, the standardized death rate in the families of the employed between 1931 and 1934 was 21.01 deaths per 1000 but 29.29 per 1000 among the families of the unemployed. Interpret-ation of this and similar material seems obvious, but to err on the side of caution we must note the possibility that those already in poor health were more likely than the healthy to become and to stay unemployed, so it is not absolutely certain, merely highly probable, that unemployment caused health to deteriorate. The evidence seems more certain that women and children especially suffered. The Save the Children Fund team reported more malnu-trition in 1932 than in 1931 following the cuts in pay and un-employment benefits that year, and some local medical officers confirmed this. Women suffered in two ways, firstly because wives tended to cut back on their own consumption of food in order to feed children and husbands first, and secondly because in pregnancy their need for expensive foods like milk, fish and fresh vegetables increased, but their income did not. Indeed, the re-duction in pay and benefits in the early 1930s may explain some of that disturbing increase in rates of maternal mortality. The

Pilgrim Trust cited this as a consequence of the depression in *Men Without Work* (1938), their analysis of the social effects of unemployment [9].

If health varied according to social group, it also varied regionally. Once again national averages disguised substantial inequalities. The standardized death rate for Glamorgan in 1938 was 24 per cent above the national average for the whole of England and Wales. Within that county Merthyr Tydfil's death rate was 52 per cent above the average. In Lancashire the death rate for Wigan was 34 per cent higher, in South Shields and Jarrow in Co. Durham it was about 30 per cent higher. On the other hand the rate in Surrey was about 20 per cent below the average. The contrast in infant mortality rates is even more stark. It was better to be born in Hastings with an infant mortality rate in 1934 of 35 deaths per 1000 live births or in Oxfordshire with 38, rather than in Co. Durham with 78, Salford with 92 or Barrow-in-Furness with 98. The Ministry of Health tended to disregard the health statistics of Scotland: while the infant mortality rate in England and Wales was on average down to 58 deaths per 1000 live births in 1937, it was still at 80.3 in Scotland, 104 in Glasgow. That is an awful lot of dead babies [1, 2, 8].

Explanations of such regional inequalities may point to the less developed medical services outside London and the South East: fewer doctors, hospital beds, clinics and so on. There were also the poorer environmental conditions in the older industrial areas of northern England, southern Scotland and South Wales: the preponderance of older housing stock and the worse overcrowding in these regions have already been discussed. Many of the harder, more exhausting and more health-wrecking industrial occupations were still located in the North and Wales, in the mines, steelworks, shipyards and mills. We should not overlook the physical exhaustion induced by some industrial activities in the South and East, but it seems probable that workers in the newer industries mainly to be found in those regions worked and lived in a less hostile environment. But in addition there was the question of nutrition. The material to make simple comparisons between regional diets has not been assembled, but we do know, as explained earlier, that regional rates of unemployment varied

41

considerably between the wars and we know that unemployment usually caused a drop in family income. We also know that rates of pay were generally lower in the North and in Wales. It seems reasonable to conclude that the resulting higher preponderance of poverty in these regions affected the adequacy of diets. The consequences upon regional health seem apparent in the records.

The Ministry of Health had some reason to feel pleased by the real improvements in the nation's health between the wars. However, officials tended to suggest in the 1930s that the biological limits were being approached beyond which it would not be possible to reduce death rates. It was this complacency which justifiably embittered critics. Further substantial improvements were in fact to take place during and after the Second World War. For example, life expectancy at birth in England and Wales had risen by 1978–80 to 70.4 years for men and 76.6 years for women, and infant mortality rates had fallen still further to about 15 deaths per 1000 live births by 1977. But more obviously at the time, there was a substantial contrast between the health standards of different social groups and of different parts of the country. It was at least reasonable to suggest that the biological limits could not have been reached, and that room for further improvement would remain, until the disadvantaged came to enjoy the standard of health already reached by the healthiest social classes and healthiest parts of the country.

Conclusion

Research shows that more attention ought to be paid than has been customary to the signs of substantial improvement in social conditions between the wars. Those subordinate images of affluence are not deceitful. For the majority of the British people, life in Britain before the Second World War was a good deal better in material terms than it had been just before the First World War.

Credit for this improvement belongs only a little to the actions of governments. Most historians agree that government economic policy in the 1920s did little to help business. A return to the gold standard in 1925 at the pre-war parity was possibly harmful to British exports, and cuts in government expenditure, a balanced budget and a high bank rate were more certainly deflationary and a discouragement to industrial activity. In the 1930s a cheap money policy, lowering interest rates, was more helpful to investment, and tariffs perhaps enabled vulnerable industries to survive foreign competition. But orthodox budgetary policy remained a restraint, and neither industrial transference, rationalization schemes, Special Areas Acts nor other government measures had more than a marginal impact on stimulating economic growth until rearmament began late in the 1930s (6, 9). Extensions in state social welfare services were more important, and indeed the cost of these schemes, raised by taxation and insurance contributions from the employed, did involve a small but significant redistribution of income from the better-off to the poor. We should not forget the relief given to the unemployed, the sick, orphans, widows and the elderly. Nor should we overlook the expansion in the school medical service, in the number of maternity and child welfare clinics, in local authority environmental health measures and in the remarkable development of council house-building and the state subsidizing of private builders. But there were serious gaps and inadequacies in some of these services and most of them directly affected only limited numbers of people. As noted, council housing benefited a restricted class of families, state health insurance covered only wage-earners, large numbers of mothers and infants did not attend welfare clinics. Moreover, as Rowntree discovered, the more dependent families were on state welfare relief for their income the deeper was their poverty. Old age pensioners and families living on unemployment assistance were particularly hard pressed (13). Welfare services did provide a safety net beneath the British people, and between the wars it became a much better one than in the past, but it was still slung very low and, as is the nature of nets, it had holes in it.

More important in improving social conditions for the great majority of families was continued demographic change, most obviously the fall in the birth rate which reduced the burden on the average family's income. This development owed nothing to government which in fact generally discouraged the official propagation of birth-control knowledge and advice. But above all, improvement was due to the acceleration in the pace of

43

economic growth and the distribution of the consequent increased wealth to the great bulk of the British people. This growth was mainly the fruit of the hard work and skills of the manual and non-manual labour force, technical ingenuity and entrepreneurial initiative.

It was this growth in particular which made possible higher family earnings. Increased purchases of food and consumer goods, better housing and the enjoyment of a wider range of leisure activities were natural consequences. On average, the nation was physically fitter by 1939, if only for war. There are also signs that this prosperity was ushering in a more homogeneous national culture, crossing class and regional lines. A national British Broadcasting Corporation, for example, may have induced a greater sense of national unity, passing on to the mass public, which could now afford radios and licences, items of national news, the jokes of national comedians and even, in 1936, national bulletins on a dying king. More people were buying the same national daily and Sunday newspapers, absorbing similar information and ideas, reading and responding to the same advertisements pressing similar habits of consumption upon them. More people lived in similar-style houses, ate similarly processed, packaged and marketed foodstuffs, stood shoulder to shoulder to watch the same or similar football matches and queued together to see the same Gracie Fields film.

Seen in conjunction with the simultaneous restructuring of British industry and the significant shifts of investment and employment out of the old and into the new, interwar Britain appears an important time of transition, a pivot between two periods. Some of the social and cultural conventions of Victorian society departed with much of its industry, its housing and its social conditions. Britain was moving and apparently with speed towards the affluent mass consumer society she became after the Second World War.

We should not ignore the cost of this transition. This was a painful process of change. Even rehousing was not without its destructive side when emigrants to the suburbs left the anchorage of well-established neighbourhoods. The restructuring of industry especially brought its casualties when the large staple industries were trimmed to fit reduced market needs. Those who had invested most in the past suffered most in the present. Working-class communities which had single-mindedly invested their labour in the local staple industry, such as the mining towns and villages of South Wales and Co. Durham, had most to lose. But throughout the older industrial areas, industrial restructuring destroyed jobs, made skills redundant and caused psychological suffering at least as serious as the decline in material living standards. Those popular images of depression and decay are not false and are themselves part of the reality of interwar Britain. And as noted, this shift reversed the basic nineteenth-century pattern and returned the balance of economic opportunity in favour of London and the South.

While this was an age of change causing discontinuities, the historian must remain aware of the continuities. After all, regional inequality in living standards was itself not new. Nor was class inequality. There are a few signs that the distribution of national income became a little more equal than before 1914, with a slight raising up at the bottom of society and a slight flattening out at the top. But otherwise the social pyramid remained broadly unchanged. It is salutary to remember that in 1936 a mere 5 per cent of the population of England and Wales aged over 25 owned some 81 per cent of the nation's private capital, a proportion only marginally reduced from the level of before 1914 (7). Since income and wealth remained unequally shared, so was purchasing power. As in the past, standards of living remained unequal, with enormous variations in the level of consumer spending, in expenditure on leisure activities, in the quality of people's homes, in the food they ate, and in their health. It was therefore a comparatively prosperous but socially unequal Great Britain which went to war in 1939.

Select bibliography

(Place of publication is London unless otherwise stated)

1 C. L. Mowat, *Britain between the Wars 1918–1940* (Methuen, 1955).
2 S. Glynn and J. Oxborrow, *Interwar Britain: a Social and Economic History* (Allen & Unwin, 1976).
3 N. Branson, *Britain in the Nineteen Twenties* (Weidenfeld & Nicolson, 1975).
4 N. Branson and M. Heinemann, *Britain in the Nineteen Thirties* (Weidenfeld & Nicolson, 1971).
5 J. Stevenson and C. Cook, *The Slump: Society and Politics during the Depression* (Cape, 1977).
6 D. H. Aldcroft, *The Inter-War Economy: Britain 1919–1939* (Batsford, 1970).
   The above are general texts with extensive references to further reading.
7 A. H. Halsey (ed.), *Trends in British Society since 1900* (Macmillan, 1972).
   A valuable collection of statistical tables and commentary.
8 J. Stevenson, *Social Conditions in Britain between the Wars* (Harmondsworth, Penguin, 1977).
   Contains a useful introductory essay and substantial extracts from contemporary sources.
9 S. Constantine, *Unemployment in Britain between the Wars* (Longman, 1980).
   Causes, consequences and policies: in Longman's Seminar Studies series.
10 J. Burnett, *A Social History of Housing 1815–1970* (Methuen paperback, 1980).

11 A. A. Jackson, *Semi-Detached London* (Allen & Unwin, 1973).
   An entertaining local study for transport and housing enthusiasts.
12 J. Burnett, *Plenty and Want* (Scolar, 1979, now available from Methuen).
   A social history of diet since 1815.
13 B. S. Rowntree, *Poverty and Progress* (Longman, 1941).
14 J. B. Priestley, *English Journey* (Gollancz, 1934, reprinted by Penguin, 1977).
15 W. Greenwood, *Love on the Dole* (Cape, 1933, reprinted by Penguin, 1969).
   Three readily available contemporary works, the latter being the classic novel of life in the depressed North of England.